This is mine:

NAME: _____

PHONE: _____

ADDRESS: _____

EMAIL: _____

Copyright @ 2019 Happy Press
All Rights Reserved
ISBN: 9781070527970
Without your voice we don't exist.

Please support us and leave a review!

Thank you!

Disclaimer:

Product name, logos, brand and other trademarks featured or referred to in this publication are the property of their respective trademark holders and are not affiliated with this publication. The publisher and author make no representations or warranties with the respect to the accuracy or completeness of these contents and disclaim all warranties such as warranties of fitness for a particular purpose.

The information in this book is meant for educational and entertainment purposes only. This book is unofficial and unauthorized. It is not authorized, approved, licensed or endorsed by the original book's author or publisher and any other licensees or affiliates

MY FUTURE, MY WAY

DATE:

Personal Goals

Career Goals

New/Good Habit Tracker

For The Month Of: _____

New Habit	Color in every day you embraced your new/good habit!

Why I Want To Create these Habits:	Challenges Ahead:	30 Day Overview - How I Did!	Looking Ahead - How I Will Continue These Habits:

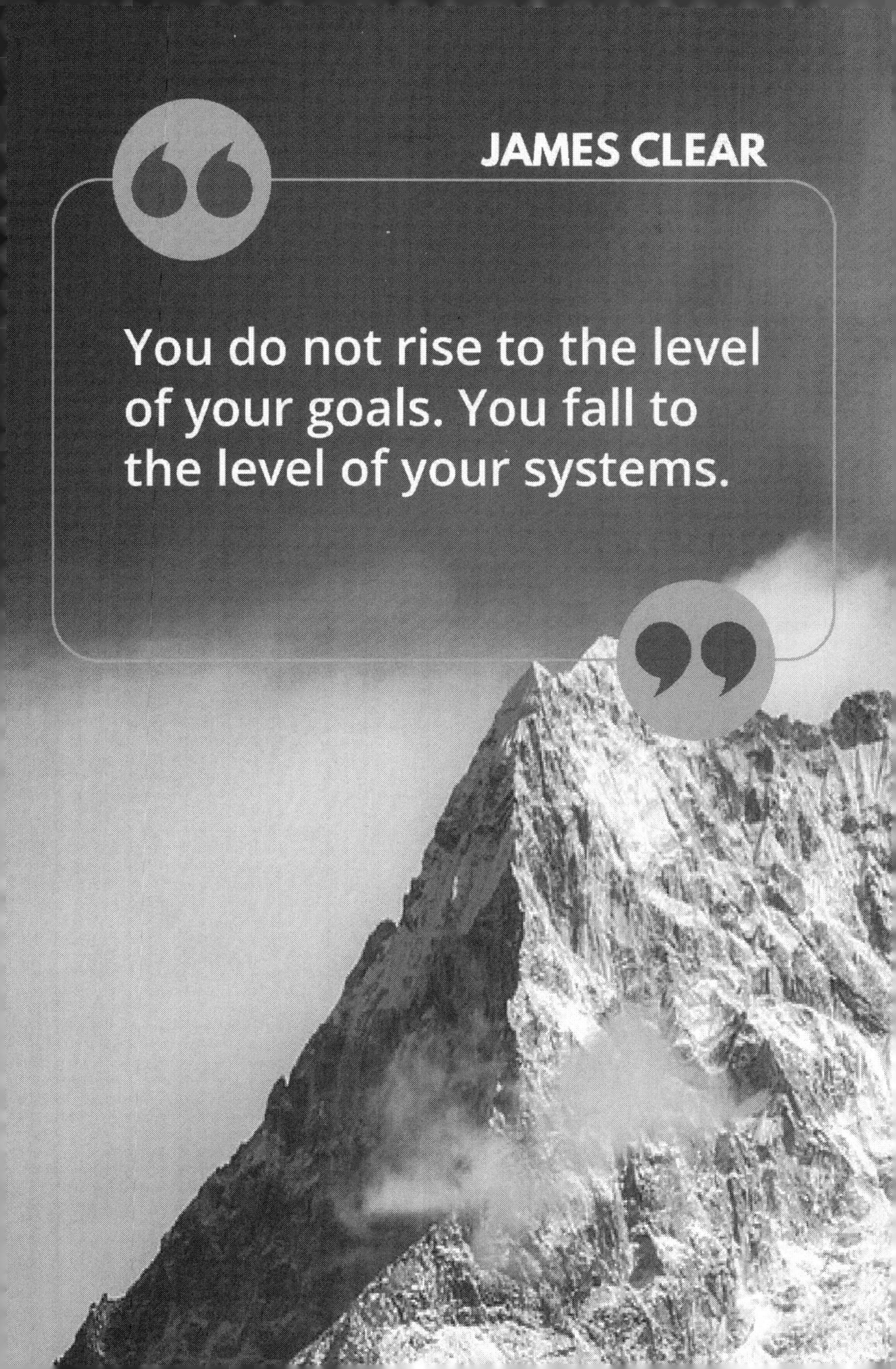

JAMES CLEAR

You do not rise to the level of your goals. You fall to the level of your systems.

Old/Bad Habit Tracker

For The Month Of: _____

Old Habit	Color in every day you avoided the old/bad habit!

Why I Want To Eliminate These Habits:	Challenges Ahead:	30 Day Overview - How I Did!	Looking Ahead - How I Will Stay On Track:

New/Good Habit Tracker

For The Month Of: _____

New Habit	Color in every day you embraced your new/good habit!

Why I Want To Create these Habits:	Challenges Ahead:	30 Day Overview - How I Did!	Looking Ahead - How I Will Continue These Habits:

Old/Bad Habit Tracker

For The Month Of: _____

Old Habit	Color in every day you avoided the old/bad habit!

Why I Want To Eliminate These Habits:	Challenges Ahead:	30 Day Overview - How I Did!	Looking Ahead - How I Will Stay On Track:

New/Good Habit Tracker

For The Month Of: _____

New Habit	Color in every day you embraced your new/good habit!

Why I Want To Create these Habits:	Challenges Ahead:	30 Day Overview - How I Did!	Looking Ahead - How I Will Continue These Habits:

Old/Bad Habit Tracker
For The Month Of: _____

Old Habit	Color in every day you avoided the old/bad habit!

Why I Want To Eliminate These Habits:	Challenges Ahead:	30 Day Overview - How I Did!	Looking Ahead - How I Will Stay On Track:

New/Good Habit Tracker

For The Month Of: _____

New Habit	Color in every day you embraced your new/good habit!

Why I Want To Create these Habits:	Challenges Ahead:	30 Day Overview - How I Did!	Looking Ahead - How I Will Continue These Habits:

Old/Bad Habit Tracker

For The Month Of: _____

Old Habit	Color in every day you avoided the old/bad habit!

Why I Want To Eliminate These Habits:	Challenges Ahead:	30 Day Overview - How I Did!	Looking Ahead - How I Will Stay On Track:

New/Good Habit Tracker

For The Month Of: _____

New Habit	Color in every day you embraced your new/good habit!

Why I Want To Create these Habits:	Challenges Ahead:	30 Day Overview - How I Did!	Looking Ahead - How I Will Continue These Habits:

Old/Bad Habit Tracker

For The Month Of: _____

Old Habit	Color in every day you avoided the old/bad habit!

Why I Want To Eliminate These Habits:	Challenges Ahead:	30 Day Overview - How I Did!	Looking Ahead - How I Will Stay On Track:

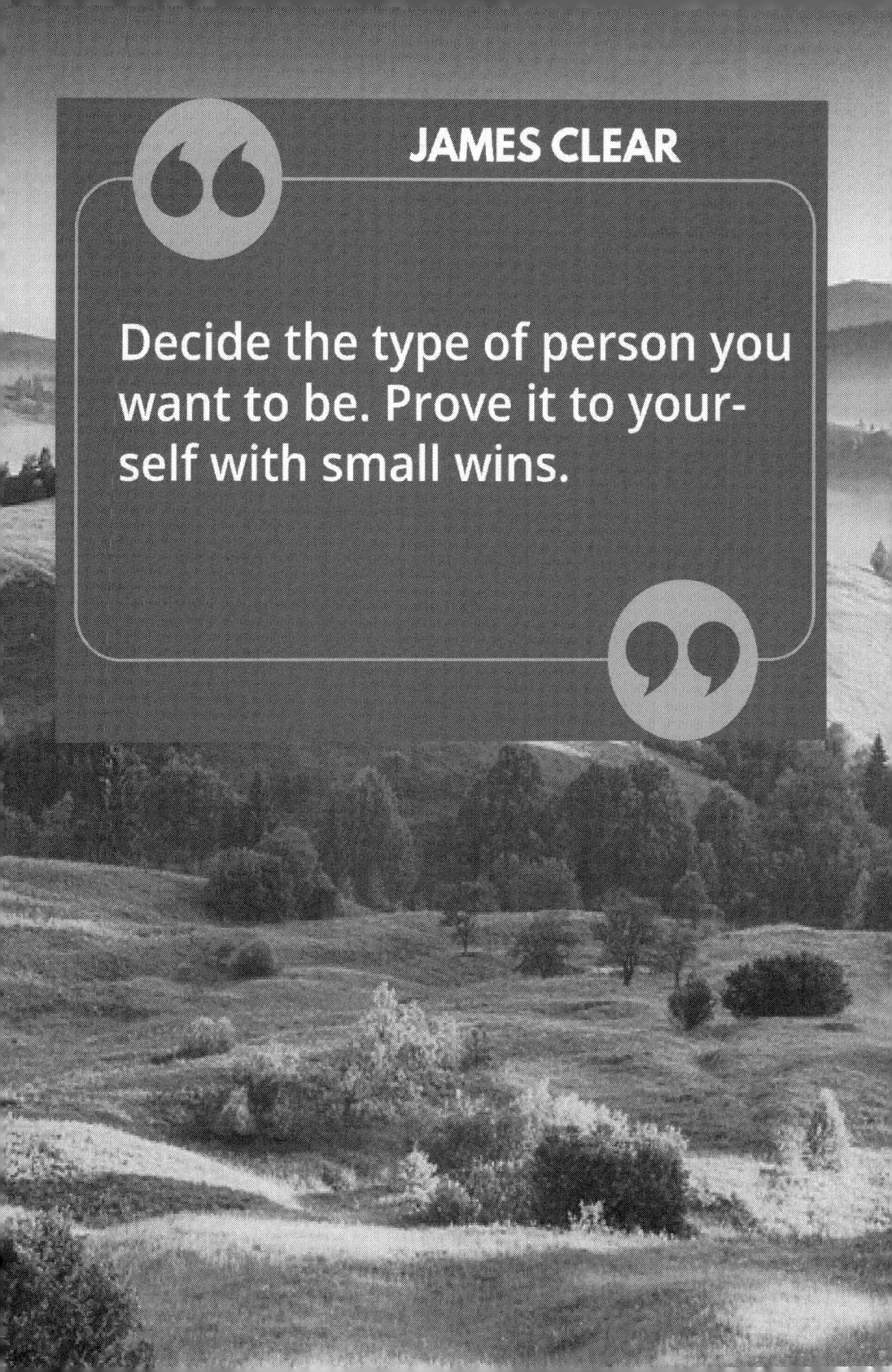

New/Good Habit Tracker

For The Month Of: _____

New Habit	Color in every day you embraced your new/good habit!

Why I Want To Create these Habits:	Challenges Ahead:	30 Day Overview - How I Did!	Looking Ahead - How I Will Continue These Habits:

Old/Bad Habit Tracker

For The Month Of: _____

Old Habit	Color in every day you avoided the old/bad habit!

Why I Want To Eliminate These Habits:	Challenges Ahead:	30 Day Overview - How I Did!	Looking Ahead - How I Will Stay On Track:

New/Good Habit Tracker

For The Month Of: _____

New Habit	Color in every day you embraced your new/good habit!

Why I Want To Create these Habits:	Challenges Ahead:	30 Day Overview - How I Did!	Looking Ahead - How I Will Continue These Habits:

Old/Bad Habit Tracker
For The Month Of: _____

Old Habit	Color in every day you avoided the old/bad habit!

Why I Want To Eliminate These Habits:	Challenges Ahead:	30 Day Overview - How I Did!	Looking Ahead - How I Will Stay On Track:

New/Good Habit Tracker

For The Month Of: _____

New Habit	Color in every day you embraced your new/good habit!

Why I Want To Create these Habits:	Challenges Ahead:	30 Day Overview - How I Did!	Looking Ahead - How I Will Continue These Habits:

Old/Bad Habit Tracker
For The Month Of: _____

Old Habit	Color in every day you avoided the old/bad habit!

Why I Want To Eliminate These Habits:	Challenges Ahead:	30 Day Overview - How I Did!	Looking Ahead - How I Will Stay On Track:

New/Good Habit Tracker

For The Month Of: _____

New Habit	Color in every day you embraced your new/good habit!

Why I Want To Create these Habits:	Challenges Ahead:	30 Day Overview - How I Did!	Looking Ahead - How I Will Continue These Habits:

Old/Bad Habit Tracker

For The Month Of: _____

Old Habit	Color in every day you avoided the old/bad habit!

Why I Want To Eliminate These Habits:	Challenges Ahead:	30 Day Overview - How I Did!	Looking Ahead - How I Will Stay On Track:

New/Good Habit Tracker

For The Month Of: _____

| New Habit | Color in every day you embraced your new/good habit! |
|---|---|ುತ

Why I Want To Create these Habits:	Challenges Ahead:	30 Day Overview - How I Did!	Looking Ahead - How I Will Continue These Habits:

> It is easy to get bogged down trying to find the optimal plan for change: the fastest way to lose weight, the best program to build muscle, the perfect idea for a side hustle. We are so focused on figuring out the best approach that we never get around to taking action.
>
> **JAMES CLEAR**

Old/Bad Habit Tracker

For The Month Of: _____

Old Habit	Color in every day you avoided the old/bad habit!

Why I Want To Eliminate These Habits:	Challenges Ahead:	30 Day Overview - How I Did!	Looking Ahead - How I Will Stay On Track:

New/Good Habit Tracker

For The Month Of: _____

New Habit	Color in every day you embraced your new/good habit!

Why I Want To Create these Habits:	Challenges Ahead:	30 Day Overview - How I Did!	Looking Ahead - How I Will Continue These Habits:

Old/Bad Habit Tracker

For The Month Of: _____

Old Habit	Color in every day you avoided the old/bad habit!

Why I Want To Eliminate These Habits:	Challenges Ahead:	30 Day Overview - How I Did!	Looking Ahead - How I Will Stay On Track:

New/Good Habit Tracker

For The Month Of: _____

New Habit	Color in every day you embraced your new/good habit!

Why I Want To Create these Habits:	Challenges Ahead:	30 Day Overview - How I Did!	Looking Ahead - How I Will Continue These Habits:

Old/Bad Habit Tracker

For The Month Of: _____

Old Habit	Color in every day you avoided the old/bad habit!

Why I Want To Eliminate These Habits:	Challenges Ahead:	30 Day Overview - How I Did!	Looking Ahead - How I Will Stay On Track:

New/Good Habit Tracker

For The Month Of: _____

New Habit	Color in every day you embraced your new/good habit!

Why I Want To Create these Habits:	Challenges Ahead:	30 Day Overview - How I Did!	Looking Ahead - How I Will Continue These Habits:

Old/Bad Habit Tracker

For The Month Of: _____

Old Habit	Color in every day you avoided the old/bad habit!

Why I Want To Eliminate These Habits:	Challenges Ahead:	30 Day Overview - How I Did!	Looking Ahead - How I Will Stay On Track:

New/Good Habit Tracker

For The Month Of: _____

New Habit	Color in every day you embraced your new/good habit!

Why I Want To Create these Habits:	Challenges Ahead:	30 Day Overview - How I Did!	Looking Ahead - How I Will Continue These Habits:

Old/Bad Habit Tracker

For The Month Of: _____

Old Habit	Color in every day you avoided the old/bad habit!

Why I Want To Eliminate These Habits:	Challenges Ahead:	30 Day Overview - How I Did!	Looking Ahead - How I Will Stay On Track:

> We often dismiss small changes because they don't seem to matter very much in the moment.

JAMES CLEAR

New/Good Habit Tracker

For The Month Of: _____

New Habit	Color in every day you embraced your new/good habit!

Why I Want To Create these Habits:	Challenges Ahead:	30 Day Overview - How I Did!	Looking Ahead - How I Will Continue These Habits:

Old/Bad Habit Tracker
For The Month Of: _____

Old Habit	Color in every day you avoided the old/bad habit!

Why I Want To Eliminate These Habits:	Challenges Ahead:	30 Day Overview - How I Did!	Looking Ahead - How I Will Stay On Track:

New/Good Habit Tracker

For The Month Of: _____

New Habit	Color in every day you embraced your new/good habit!

Why I Want To Create these Habits:	Challenges Ahead:	30 Day Overview - How I Did!	Looking Ahead - How I Will Continue These Habits:

Old/Bad Habit Tracker
For The Month Of: _____

Old Habit	Color in every day you avoided the old/bad habit!

Why I Want To Eliminate These Habits:	Challenges Ahead:	30 Day Overview - How I Did!	Looking Ahead - How I Will Stay On Track:

New/Good Habit Tracker

For The Month Of: _____

New Habit	Color in every day you embraced your new/good habit!

Why I Want To Create these Habits:	Challenges Ahead:	30 Day Overview - How I Did!	Looking Ahead - How I Will Continue These Habits:

Old/Bad Habit Tracker
For The Month Of: _____

Old Habit	Color in every day you avoided the old/bad habit!

Why I Want To Eliminate These Habits:	Challenges Ahead:	30 Day Overview - How I Did!	Looking Ahead - How I Will Stay On Track:

New/Good Habit Tracker

For The Month Of: _____

New Habit	Color in every day you embraced your new/good habit!

Why I Want To Create these Habits:	Challenges Ahead:	30 Day Overview - How I Did!	Looking Ahead - How I Will Continue These Habits:

Old/Bad Habit Tracker

For The Month Of: _____

Old Habit	Color in every day you avoided the old/bad habit!

Why I Want To Eliminate These Habits:	Challenges Ahead:	30 Day Overview - How I Did!	Looking Ahead - How I Will Stay On Track:

New/Good Habit Tracker

For The Month Of: _____

New Habit	Color in every day you embraced your new/good habit!

Why I Want To Create these Habits:	Challenges Ahead:	30 Day Overview - How I Did!	Looking Ahead - How I Will Continue These Habits:

Time magnifies the margin between success and failure. It will multiply whatever you feed it. Good habits make time your ally. Bad habits make time your enemy.

JAMES CLEAR

Old/Bad Habit Tracker

For The Month Of: _____

Old Habit	Color in every day you avoided the old/bad habit!

Why I Want To Eliminate These Habits:	Challenges Ahead:	30 Day Overview - How I Did!	Looking Ahead - How I Will Stay On Track:

New/Good Habit Tracker

For The Month Of: _____

New Habit	Color in every day you embraced your new/good habit!

Why I Want To Create these Habits:	Challenges Ahead:	30 Day Overview - How I Did!	Looking Ahead - How I Will Continue These Habits:

Old/Bad Habit Tracker

For The Month Of: _____

Old Habit	Color in every day you avoided the old/bad habit!

Why I Want To Eliminate These Habits:	Challenges Ahead:	30 Day Overview - How I Did!	Looking Ahead - How I Will Stay On Track:

New/Good Habit Tracker

For The Month Of: _____

New Habit	Color in every day you embraced your new/good habit!

Why I Want To Create these Habits:	Challenges Ahead:	30 Day Overview - How I Did!	Looking Ahead - How I Will Continue These Habits:

Old/Bad Habit Tracker

For The Month Of: _____

| Old Habit | Color in every day you avoided the old/bad habit! |
|---|---|ослед
| | |

Why I Want To Eliminate These Habits:	Challenges Ahead:	30 Day Overview - How I Did!	Looking Ahead - How I Will Stay On Track:

New/Good Habit Tracker

For The Month Of: _____

New Habit	Color in every day you embraced your new/good habit!

Why I Want To Create these Habits:	Challenges Ahead:	30 Day Overview - How I Did!	Looking Ahead - How I Will Continue These Habits:

Old/Bad Habit Tracker

For The Month Of: _____

Old Habit	Color in every day you avoided the old/bad habit!

Why I Want To Eliminate These Habits:	Challenges Ahead:	30 Day Overview - How I Did!	Looking Ahead - How I Will Stay On Track:

New/Good Habit Tracker

For The Month Of: _____

New Habit	Color in every day you embraced your new/good habit!

Why I Want To Create these Habits:	Challenges Ahead:	30 Day Overview - How I Did!	Looking Ahead - How I Will Continue These Habits:

Old/Bad Habit Tracker

For The Month Of: _____

Old Habit	Color in every day you avoided the old/bad habit!

Why I Want To Eliminate These Habits:	Challenges Ahead:	30 Day Overview - How I Did!	Looking Ahead - How I Will Stay On Track:

It's only by making the fundamentals of life easier that you can create the mental space needed for free thinking and creativity.

JAMES CLEAR

New/Good Habit Tracker

For The Month Of: _____

New Habit	Color in every day you embraced your new/good habit!

Why I Want To Create these Habits:	Challenges Ahead:	30 Day Overview - How I Did!	Looking Ahead - How I Will Continue These Habits:

Old/Bad Habit Tracker

For The Month Of: _____

Old Habit	Color in every day you avoided the old/bad habit!

Why I Want To Eliminate These Habits:	Challenges Ahead:	30 Day Overview - How I Did!	Looking Ahead - How I Will Stay On Track:

New/Good Habit Tracker

For The Month Of: _____

New Habit	Color in every day you embraced your new/good habit!

Why I Want To Create these Habits:	Challenges Ahead:	30 Day Overview - How I Did!	Looking Ahead - How I Will Continue These Habits:

Old/Bad Habit Tracker

For The Month Of: _____

Old Habit	Color in every day you avoided the old/bad habit!

Why I Want To Eliminate These Habits:	Challenges Ahead:	30 Day Overview - How I Did!	Looking Ahead - How I Will Stay On Track:

New/Good Habit Tracker

For The Month Of: _____

New Habit	Color in every day you embraced your new/good habit!

Why I Want To Create these Habits:	Challenges Ahead:	30 Day Overview - How I Did!	Looking Ahead - How I Will Continue These Habits:

Old/Bad Habit Tracker

For The Month Of: _____

Old Habit	Color in every day you avoided the old/bad habit!

Why I Want To Eliminate These Habits:	Challenges Ahead:	30 Day Overview - How I Did!	Looking Ahead - How I Will Stay On Track:

New/Good Habit Tracker

For The Month Of: _____

New Habit	Color in every day you embraced your new/good habit!

Why I Want To Create these Habits:	Challenges Ahead:	30 Day Overview - How I Did!	Looking Ahead - How I Will Continue These Habits:

Old/Bad Habit Tracker
For The Month Of: _____

Old Habit	Color in every day you avoided the old/bad habit!

Why I Want To Eliminate These Habits:	Challenges Ahead:	30 Day Overview - How I Did!	Looking Ahead - How I Will Stay On Track:

New/Good Habit Tracker

For The Month Of: _____

New Habit	Color in every day you embraced your new/good habit!

Why I Want To Create these Habits:	Challenges Ahead:	30 Day Overview - How I Did!	Looking Ahead - How I Will Continue These Habits:

One of the most effective things you can do to build better habits is to join a culture where your desired behavior is the normal behavior.

JAMES CLEAR

Old/Bad Habit Tracker

For The Month Of: _____

Old Habit	Color in every day you avoided the old/bad habit!

Why I Want To Eliminate These Habits:	Challenges Ahead:	30 Day Overview - How I Did!	Looking Ahead - How I Will Stay On Track:

New/Good Habit Tracker

For The Month Of: _____

New Habit	Color in every day you embraced your new/good habit!

Why I Want To Create these Habits:	Challenges Ahead:	30 Day Overview - How I Did!	Looking Ahead - How I Will Continue These Habits:

Old/Bad Habit Tracker

For The Month Of: _____

Old Habit	Color in every day you avoided the old/bad habit!

Why I Want To Eliminate These Habits:	Challenges Ahead:	30 Day Overview - How I Did!	Looking Ahead - How I Will Stay On Track:

New/Good Habit Tracker

For The Month Of: _____

New Habit	Color in every day you embraced your new/good habit!

Why I Want To Create these Habits:	Challenges Ahead:	30 Day Overview - How I Did!	Looking Ahead - How I Will Continue These Habits:

Old/Bad Habit Tracker

For The Month Of: _____

Old Habit	Color in every day you avoided the old/bad habit!

Why I Want To Eliminate These Habits:	Challenges Ahead:	30 Day Overview - How I Did!	Looking Ahead - How I Will Stay On Track:

New/Good Habit Tracker

For The Month Of: _____

New Habit	Color in every day you embraced your new/good habit!

Why I Want To Create these Habits:	Challenges Ahead:	30 Day Overview - How I Did!	Looking Ahead - How I Will Continue These Habits:

Old/Bad Habit Tracker

For The Month Of: _____

Old Habit	Color in every day you avoided the old/bad habit!

Why I Want To Eliminate These Habits:	Challenges Ahead:	30 Day Overview - How I Did!	Looking Ahead - How I Will Stay On Track:

New/Good Habit Tracker

For The Month Of: _____

New Habit	Color in every day you embraced your new/good habit!

Why I Want To Create these Habits:	Challenges Ahead:	30 Day Overview - How I Did!	Looking Ahead - How I Will Continue These Habits:

Old/Bad Habit Tracker

For The Month Of: _____

Old Habit	Color in every day you avoided the old/bad habit!

Why I Want To Eliminate These Habits:	Challenges Ahead:	30 Day Overview - How I Did!	Looking Ahead - How I Will Stay On Track:

> Before we can effectively build new habits, we need to get a handle on our current ones.
>
> - James Clear

New/Good Habit Tracker

For The Month Of: _____

New Habit	Color in every day you embraced your new/good habit!

Why I Want To Create these Habits:	Challenges Ahead:	30 Day Overview - How I Did!	Looking Ahead - How I Will Continue These Habits:

Old/Bad Habit Tracker

For The Month Of: _____

Old Habit	Color in every day you avoided the old/bad habit!

Why I Want To Eliminate These Habits:	Challenges Ahead:	30 Day Overview - How I Did!	Looking Ahead - How I Will Stay On Track:

New/Good Habit Tracker

For The Month Of: _____

New Habit	Color in every day you embraced your new/good habit!

Why I Want To Create these Habits:	Challenges Ahead:	30 Day Overview - How I Did!	Looking Ahead - How I Will Continue These Habits:

Old/Bad Habit Tracker

For The Month Of: _____

Old Habit	Color in every day you avoided the old/bad habit!

Why I Want To Eliminate These Habits:	Challenges Ahead:	30 Day Overview - How I Did!	Looking Ahead - How I Will Stay On Track:

New/Good Habit Tracker

For The Month Of: _____

| New Habit | Color in every day you embraced your new/good habit! |
|---|---|//

Why I Want To Create these Habits:	Challenges Ahead:	30 Day Overview - How I Did!	Looking Ahead - How I Will Continue These Habits:

Old/Bad Habit Tracker

For The Month Of: _____

Old Habit	Color in every day you avoided the old/bad habit!

Why I Want To Eliminate These Habits:	Challenges Ahead:	30 Day Overview - How I Did!	Looking Ahead - How I Will Stay On Track:

New/Good Habit Tracker

For The Month Of: _____

New Habit	Color in every day you embraced your new/good habit!

Why I Want To Create these Habits:	Challenges Ahead:	30 Day Overview - How I Did!	Looking Ahead - How I Will Continue These Habits:

Old/Bad Habit Tracker

For The Month Of: _____

Old Habit	Color in every day you avoided the old/bad habit!

Why I Want To Eliminate These Habits:	Challenges Ahead:	30 Day Overview - How I Did!	Looking Ahead - How I Will Stay On Track:

New/Good Habit Tracker

For The Month Of: _____

New Habit	Color in every day you embraced your new/good habit!

Why I Want To Create these Habits:	Challenges Ahead:	30 Day Overview - How I Did!	Looking Ahead - How I Will Continue These Habits:

Old/Bad Habit Tracker

For The Month Of: _____

Old Habit	Color in every day you avoided the old/bad habit!

Why I Want To Eliminate These Habits:	Challenges Ahead:	30 Day Overview - How I Did!	Looking Ahead - How I Will Stay On Track:

New/Good Habit Tracker

For The Month Of: _____

New Habit	Color in every day you embraced your new/good habit!

Why I Want To Create these Habits:	Challenges Ahead:	30 Day Overview - How I Did!	Looking Ahead - How I Will Continue These Habits:

Old/Bad Habit Tracker

For The Month Of: _____

Old Habit	Color in every day you avoided the old/bad habit!

Why I Want To Eliminate These Habits:	Challenges Ahead:	30 Day Overview - How I Did!	Looking Ahead - How I Will Stay On Track:

New/Good Habit Tracker

For The Month Of: _____

New Habit	Color in every day you embraced your new/good habit!

Why I Want To Create these Habits:	Challenges Ahead:	30 Day Overview - How I Did!	Looking Ahead - How I Will Continue These Habits:

Old/Bad Habit Tracker

For The Month Of: _____

Old Habit	Color in every day you avoided the old/bad habit!

Why I Want To Eliminate These Habits:	Challenges Ahead:	30 Day Overview - How I Did!	Looking Ahead - How I Will Stay On Track:

New/Good Habit Tracker

For The Month Of: _____

New Habit	Color in every day you embraced your new/good habit!

Why I Want To Create these Habits:	Challenges Ahead:	30 Day Overview - How I Did!	Looking Ahead - How I Will Continue These Habits:

Old/Bad Habit Tracker

For The Month Of: _____

Old Habit	Color in every day you avoided the old/bad habit!

Why I Want To Eliminate These Habits:	Challenges Ahead:	30 Day Overview - How I Did!	Looking Ahead - How I Will Stay On Track:

New/Good Habit Tracker

For The Month Of: _____

New Habit	Color in every day you embraced your new/good habit!

Why I Want To Create these Habits:	Challenges Ahead:	30 Day Overview - How I Did!	Looking Ahead - How I Will Continue These Habits:

Old/Bad Habit Tracker

For The Month Of: _____

Old Habit	Color in every day you avoided the old/bad habit!

Why I Want To Eliminate These Habits:	Challenges Ahead:	30 Day Overview - How I Did!	Looking Ahead - How I Will Stay On Track:

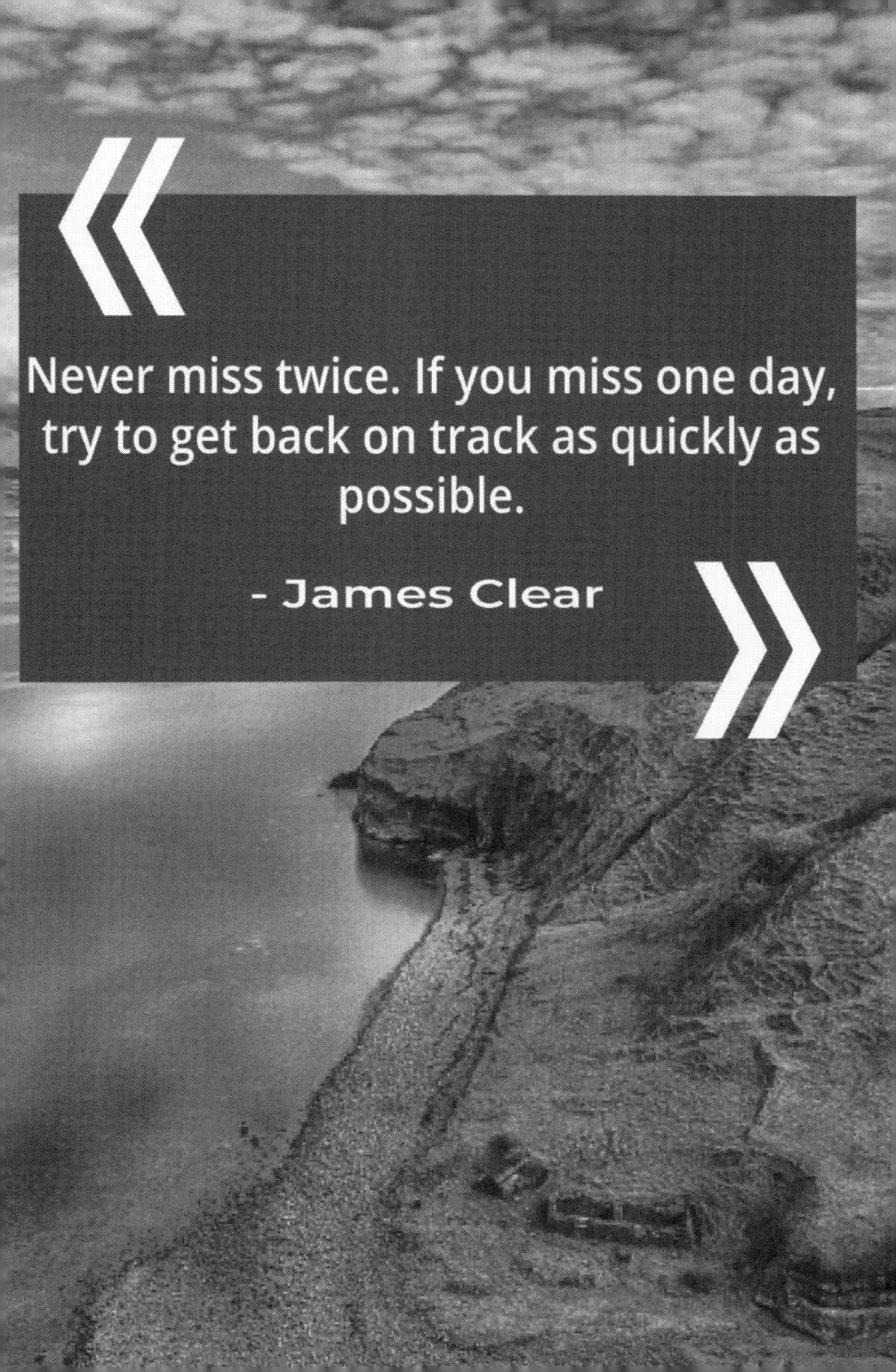

New/Good Habit Tracker

For The Month Of: _____

New Habit	Color in every day you embraced your new/good habit!

Why I Want To Create these Habits:

Challenges Ahead:

30 Day Overview - How I Did!

Looking Ahead - How I Will Continue These Habits:

Old/Bad Habit Tracker

For The Month Of: _____

Old Habit	Color in every day you avoided the old/bad habit!

Why I Want To Eliminate These Habits:	Challenges Ahead:	30 Day Overview - How I Did!	Looking Ahead - How I Will Stay On Track:

New/Good Habit Tracker

For The Month Of: _____

New Habit	Color in every day you embraced your new/good habit!

Why I Want To Create these Habits:	Challenges Ahead:	30 Day Overview - How I Did!	Looking Ahead - How I Will Continue These Habits:

Old/Bad Habit Tracker

For The Month Of: _____

Old Habit	Color in every day you avoided the old/bad habit!

Why I Want To Eliminate These Habits:	Challenges Ahead:	30 Day Overview - How I Did!	Looking Ahead - How I Will Stay On Track:

Notes

Notes

Notes

Manufactured by Amazon.ca
Bolton, ON